draw around and astound!
HOW TO DRAW
ANIMALS

Written by Elizabeth Golding

Illustrated by Hui Yuan Chang

Designed by Anton Poitier

BARRON'S

Let's get started!

This book shows you how to draw animals by drawing around shapes. All the shapes you need are at the back of the book. There are steps to draw every animal. There are also lots of hints and tips for making your drawings different!

Press out the shapes in the boards at the back of the book as you need them. They are labeled.

You can also use the press out sheet as a stencil. This is handy for the small parts, such as tails.

Start drawing!

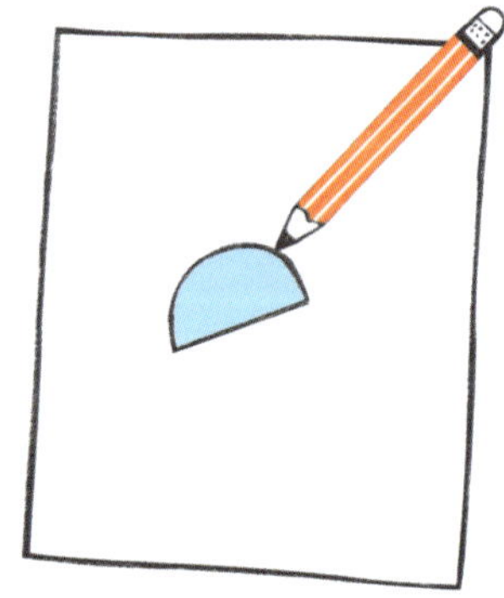 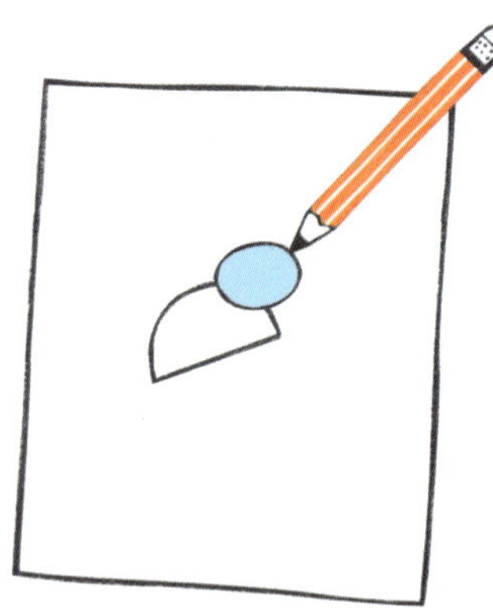 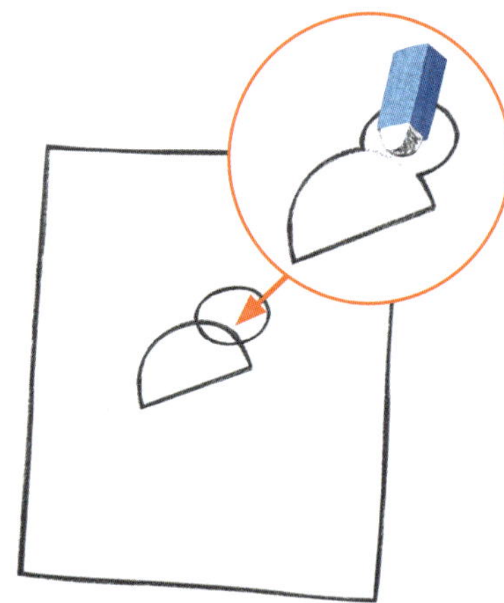

1 Begin by placing the first shape in the center of a piece of paper.

2 Place the second shape where shown, and draw around it with a pencil.

3 Use an eraser to remove the pencil marks where they go over the shape underneath.

Tips to make your animal special

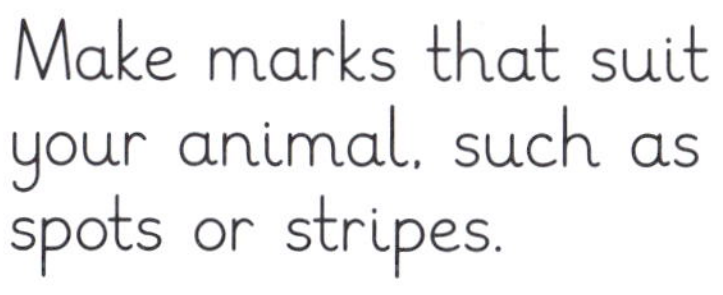

Make marks that suit your animal, such as spots or stripes.

Draw whiskers.

Use one main color for the body.

Add funny details.

Add details, such as paws, eyes, and whiskers.

Instead of using white paper, you could use colored paper. Cut it out and paste it down to make your picture.

Coloring your pictures

Here are some handy tips. You can use colored pencils, felt-tip pens, crayons, or watercolor paint to complete your drawing. Water soluble colored pencils work very well. The pictures in this book are colored in this way.

Blend the pencil colors with water.

Paint over the pencil with water.

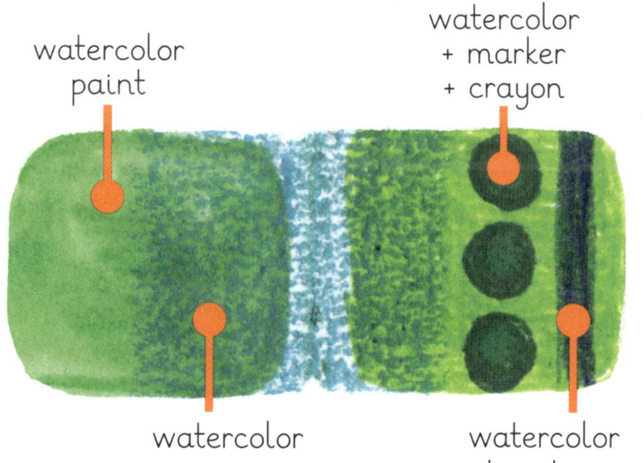

watercolor paint

watercolor + marker + crayon

watercolor + crayon

watercolor + colored pencil

Draw or paint different colors and shapes over the top of paint when it is dry.

Draw a happy dog

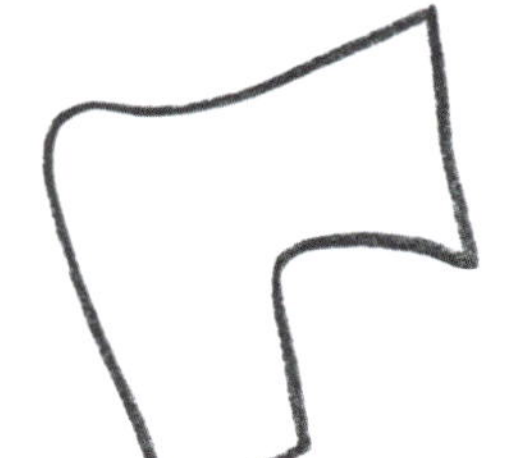

The head is facing backward.

1 Draw the dog's head.

2 Now, draw the ears.

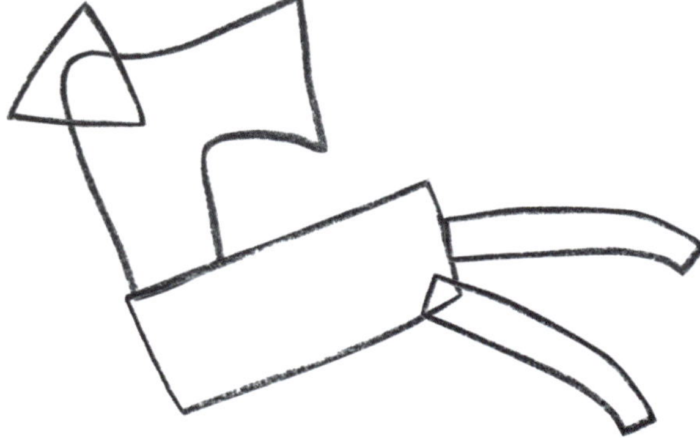

3 Add the body.

4 Draw the back legs.

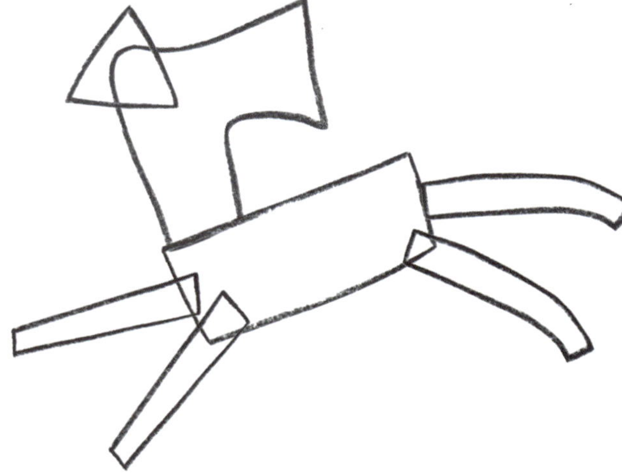

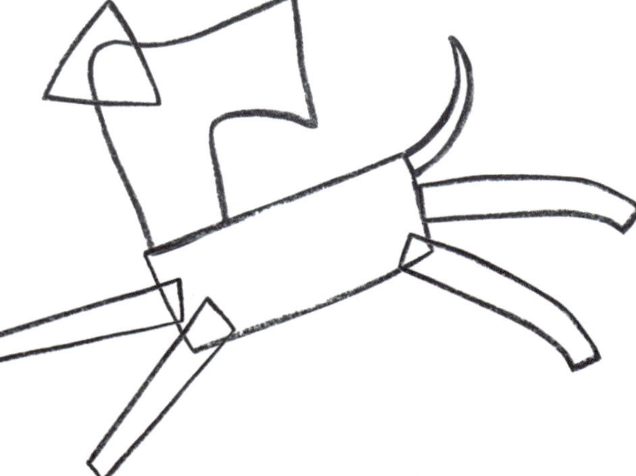

5 Add the front legs.

6 Add a curly tail.

Find the dog pieces at the back of the book. Set them out in front of you like this:

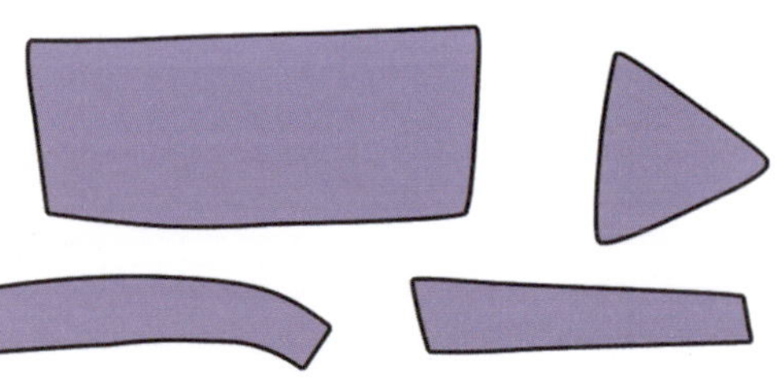

Add a collar and a ball, too!
Make your dog's tail wag!
Color your dog with paint or colored pencils.
Make your dog look different!
Give your dog a bone!
Draw the head at an angle.
Draw your dog sitting up.
Lean the body forward. Add a ball for your dog to chase!

Draw a leaping cat

Draw lightly where
lines overlap.

1 Draw the cat's head.

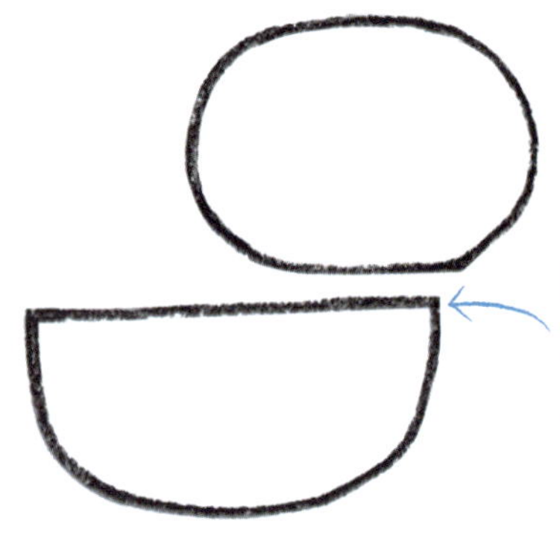

Leave a little
gap for a
collar later.

2 Add the body.

3 Now, draw the ears.

4 Draw the legs.

5 Add a curly tail.

Find the cat
pieces at the back
of the book. Set
them out in front
of you like this:

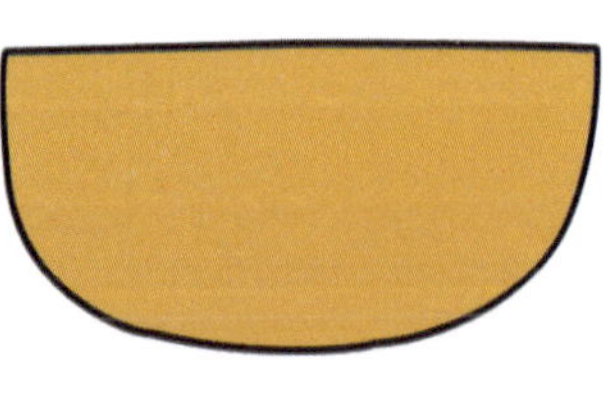

Draw a pretty pattern, then add whiskers.
Add a little mouse, too!
Make your cat look different!
Draw your cat sitting up.
Add a collar or bow tie.
Tilt the head.
Curve the tail up.
Draw straight legs.

Draw a friendly elephant

 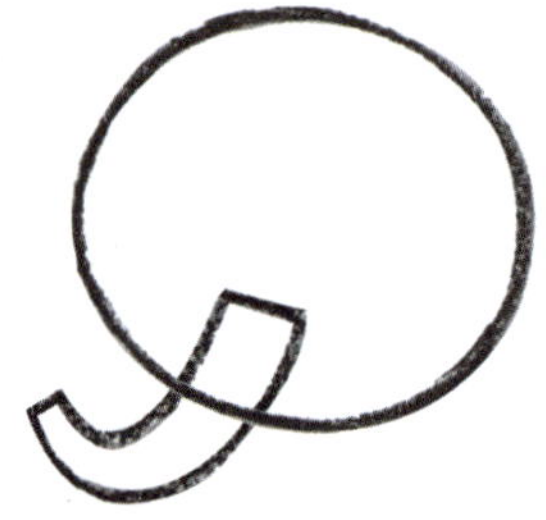

1. Draw the elephant's head. 2. Add the elephant's trunk.

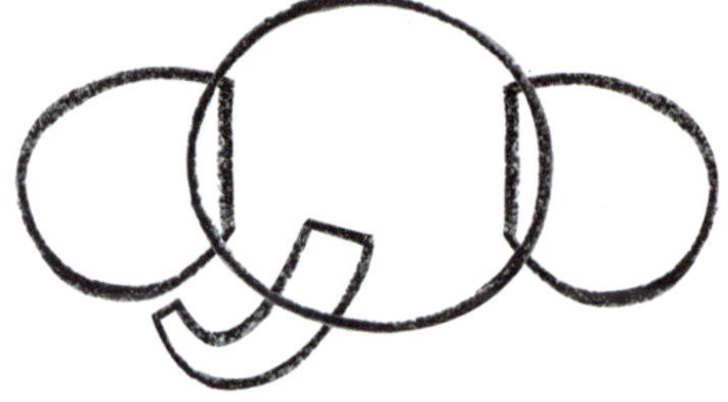 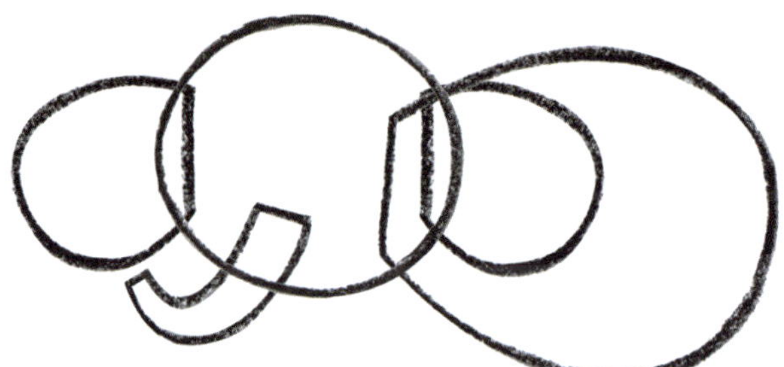

3. Draw ears on both sides. 4. Now, draw the body.

5. Draw the legs. 6. Add a swirly tail.

Find the elephant pieces at the back of the book. Set them out in front of you like this:

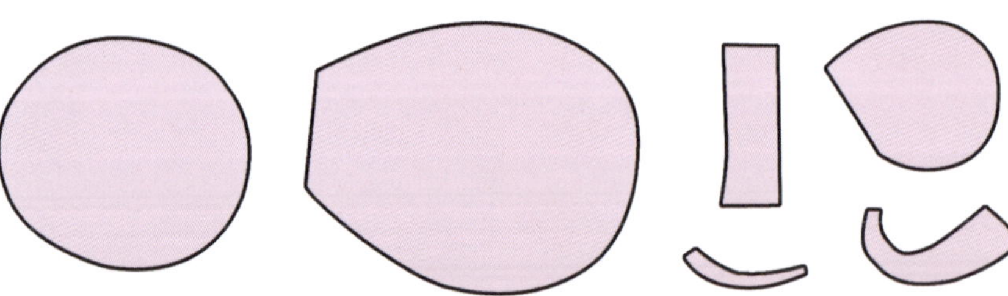

Make your elephant look different!

Arrange the pieces to draw the elephant standing up.

Show just one ear.

Show just two legs.

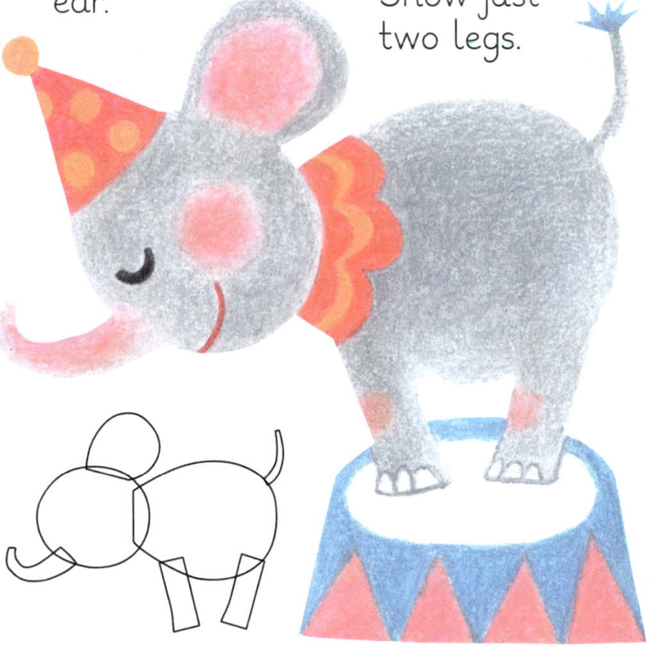

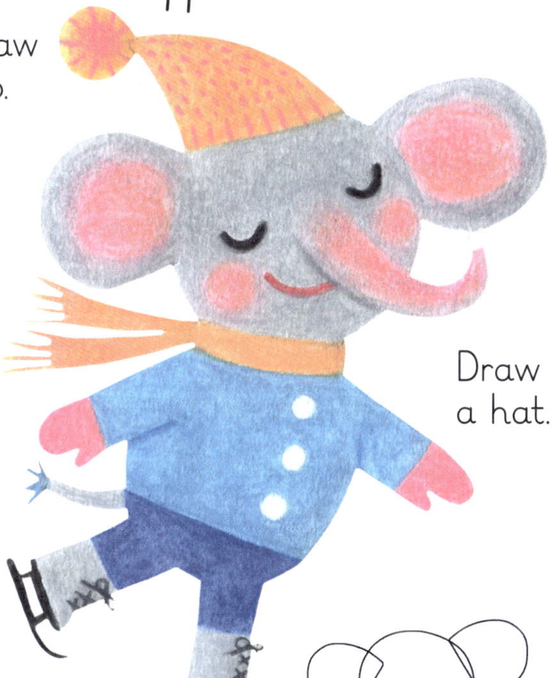

Draw a hat.

An ice skating elephant!

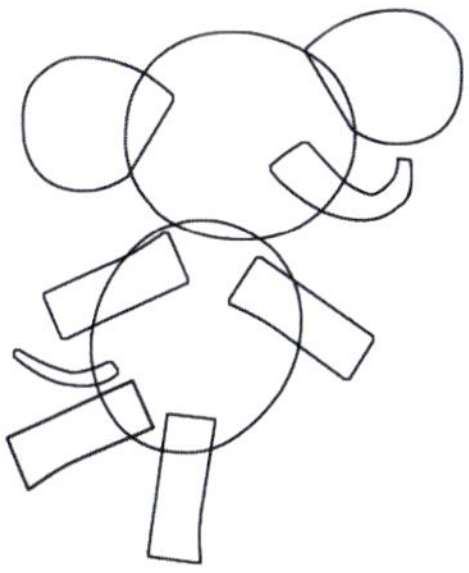

Draw a flying bird

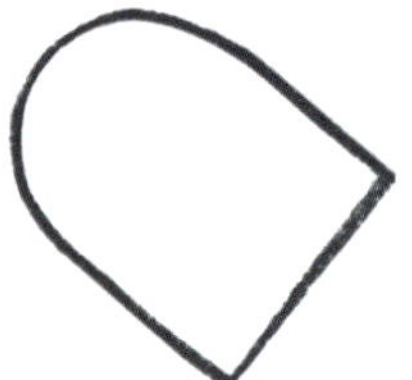

Draw lightly where lines overlap.

1. Draw the bird's head.

2. Add the body.

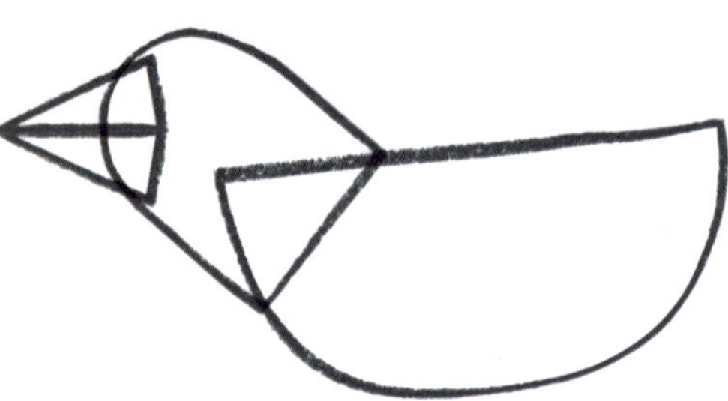

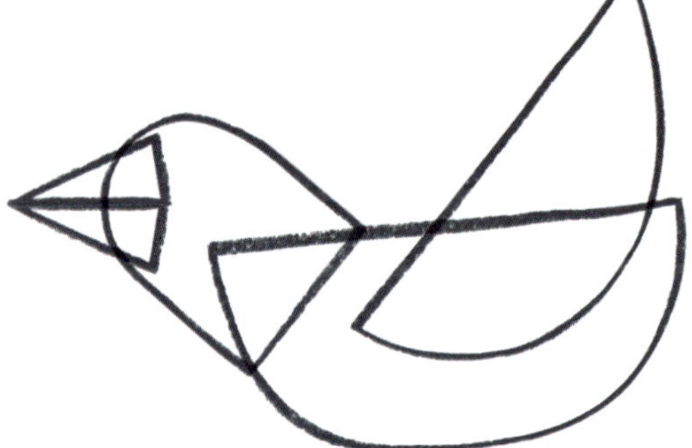

3. Now, draw the beak.

4. Draw the wing.

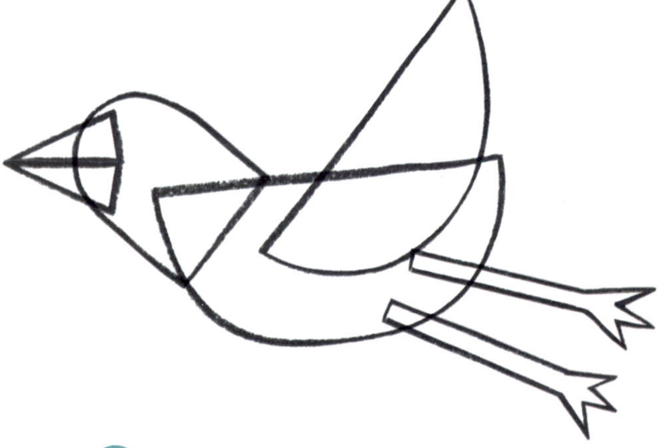

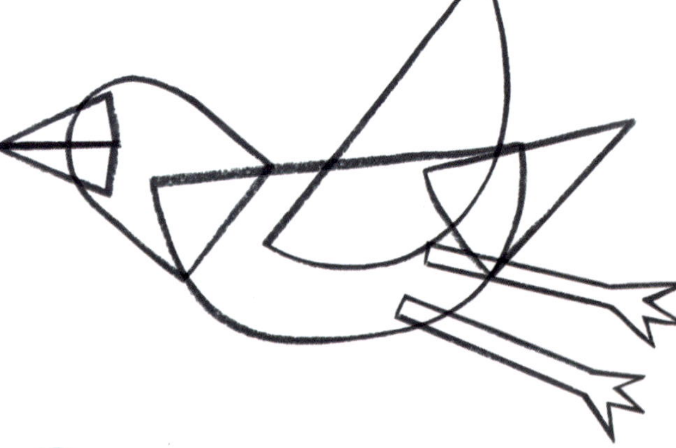

5. Add two legs.

6. Finally, draw a tail.

Find the bird pieces at the back of the book. Set them out in front of you like this:

Draw a pattern on your bird's wing and tail.
Draw the eye with a dark center.
Make your bird look different!
Add a pretty flower!
Draw the beak open and the eye closed.
Draw the legs and tail the opposite way.
Use the body shape twice to draw this bird.
Use spots and stripes.
Draw straight legs.

Draw a cute mouse

Notice the angle to draw the head.

1 Draw the mouse's head.

2 Next, draw the body.

3 Add the front paws.

4 Draw the back legs.

5 Use the stencil for the tail.

Find the mouse pieces at the back of the book. Set them out in front of you like this:

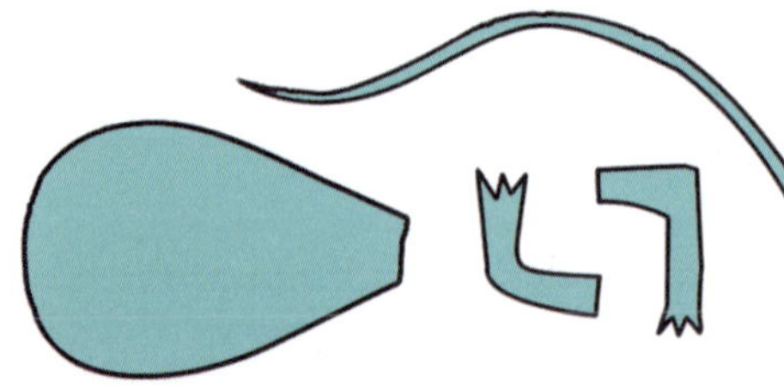

Use the stencil shape for the tail.

Draw a little friend!

Choose a color for the mouse and a different color for the face, ears, and paws.

Don't forget some whiskers!

Make your mouse look different!

Draw your mouse standing up with some cheese!

Draw a jacket and a bow tie to create a singing mouse.

Change the tail position if you draw the mouse standing.

Draw a lovely lion

Draw lightly where lines overlap.

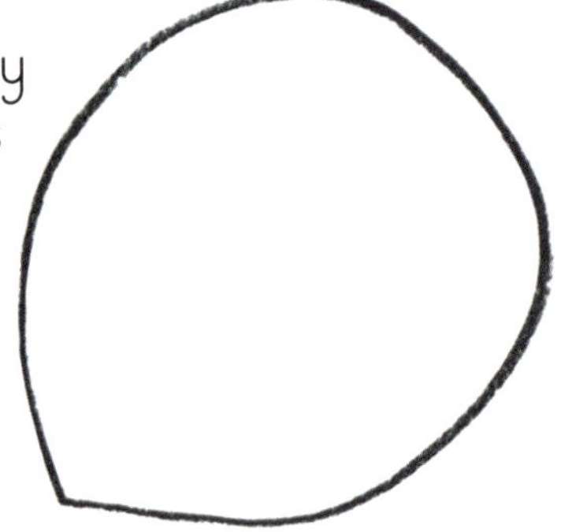

1 Draw the lion's mane.

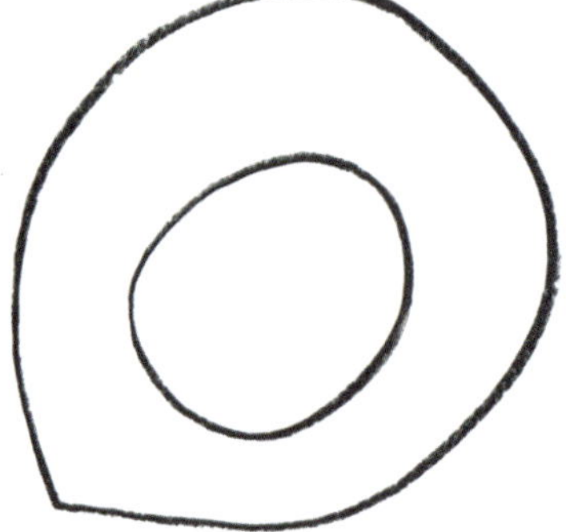

2 Draw the head next.

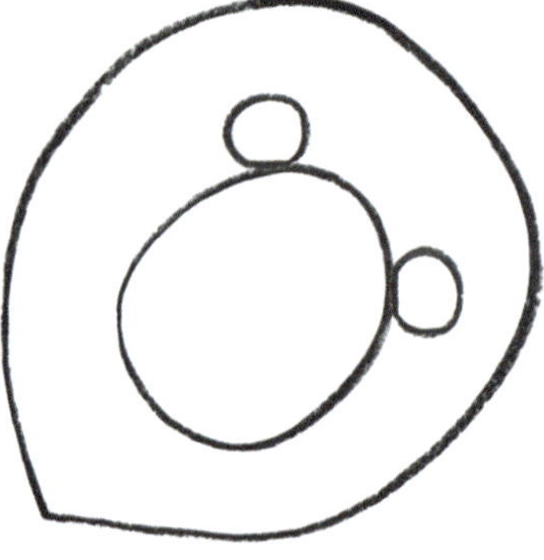

3 Now, add the ears.

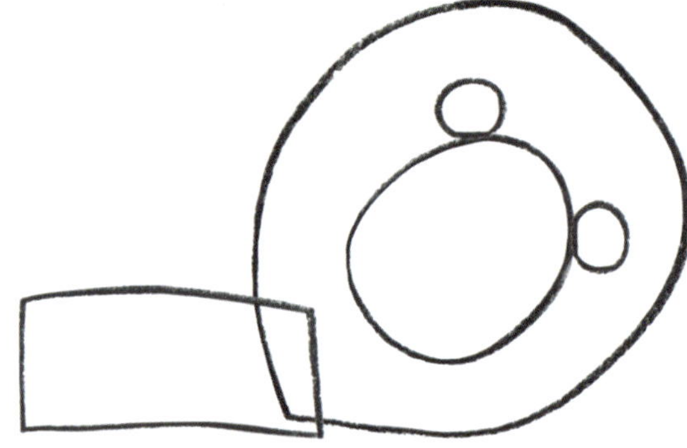

4 Add the body.

5 Add the back legs and tail.

6 Draw the front legs.

Find the lion pieces at the back of the book. Set them out in front of you like this:

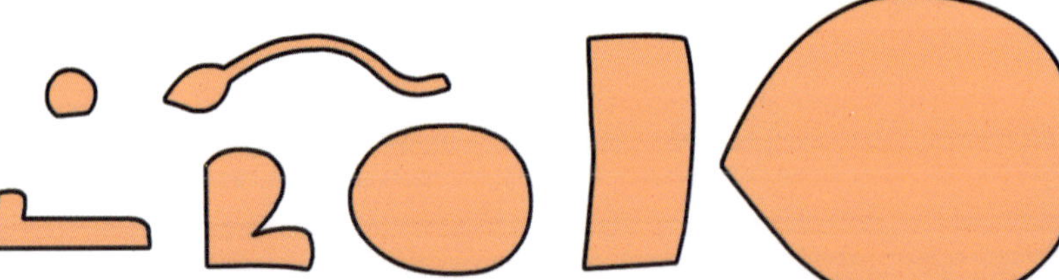

Add a little bird, too!
Leave white gaps when you color the mane.
Draw a happy face with long whiskers!
Make your lion look different!
Turn the head around and add teeth to make a fierce lion!
Tilt the head.
Draw a crown for the king of the jungle!
Draw straight legs.
Draw your lion sitting up.

Draw a jolly giraffe

Draw lightly where lines overlap.

1. Draw the giraffe's head.

2. Now, draw the body.

3. Draw the legs.

4. Add a tail.

Find the giraffe pieces at the back of the book. Set them out in front of you like this:

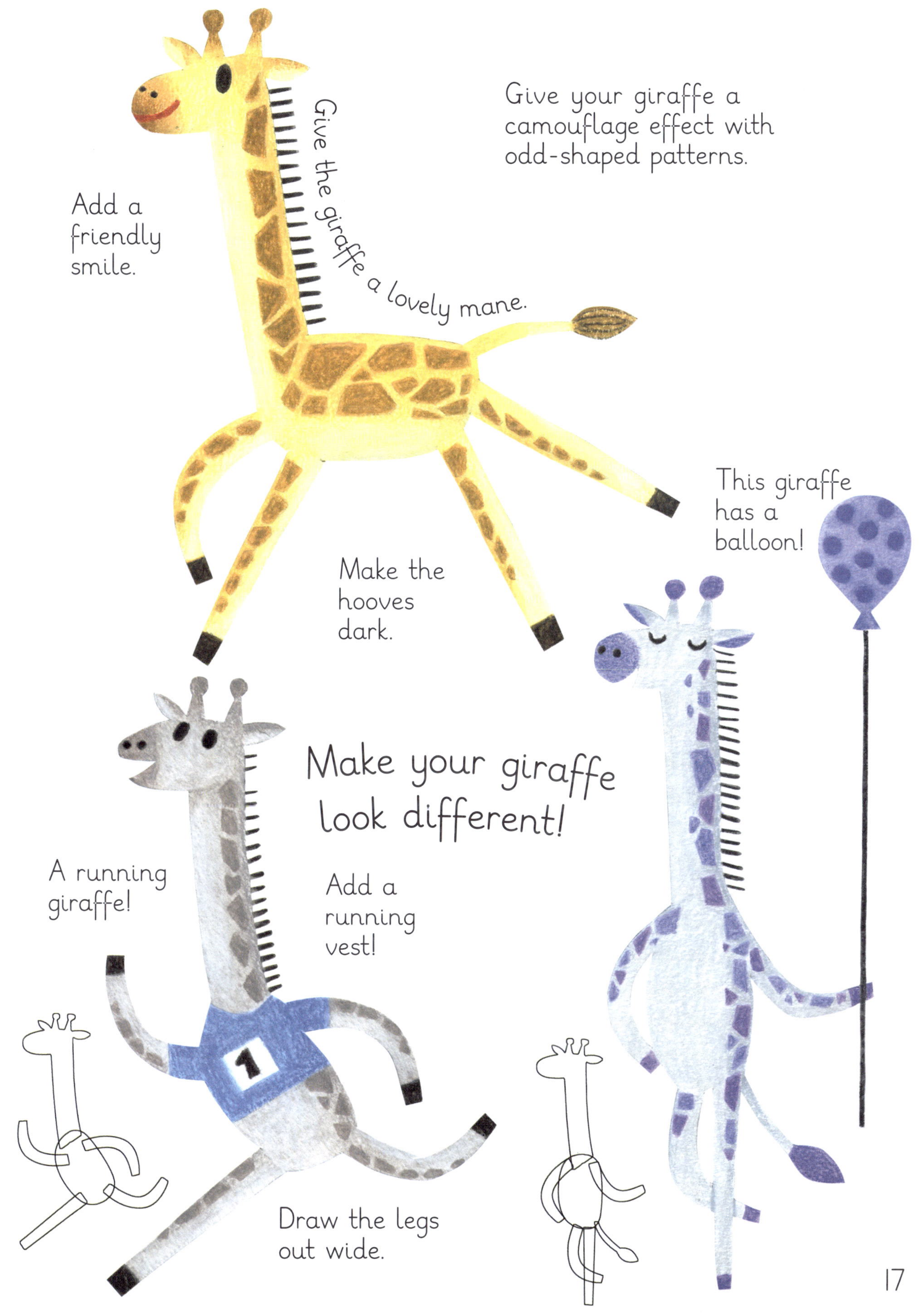

Add a friendly smile.
Give the giraffe a lovely mane.
Give your giraffe a camouflage effect with odd-shaped patterns.
This giraffe has a balloon!
Make the hooves dark.
Make your giraffe look different!
A running giraffe!
Add a running vest!
1
Draw the legs out wide.

Draw a sleepy owl

1 Draw the owl's head.

2 Add two ears.

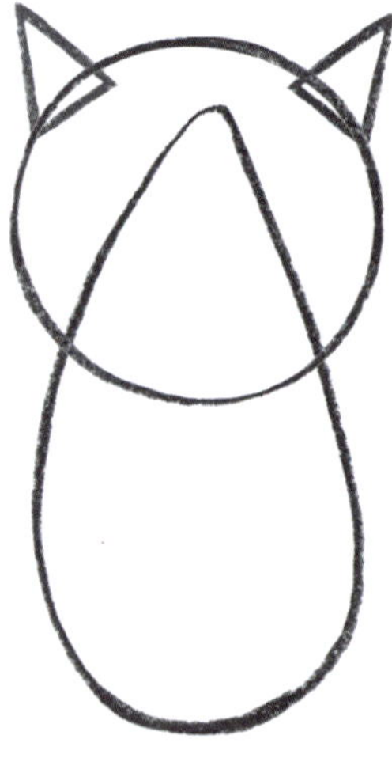

3 Now, add the body.

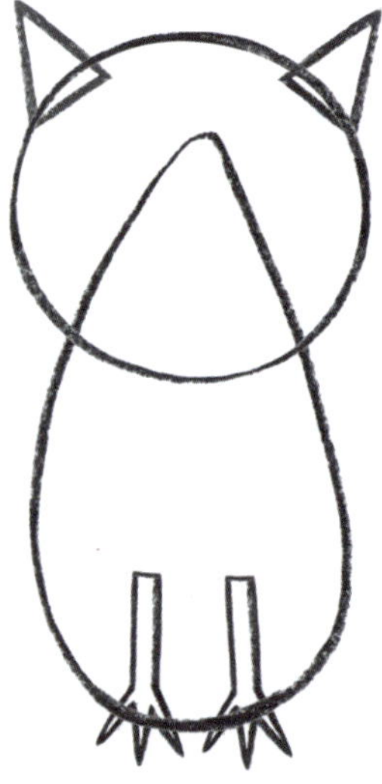

4 Draw the legs.

Find the owl pieces at the back of the book. Set them out in front of you like this:

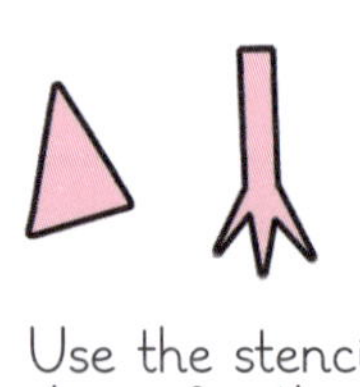

Use the stencil shape for the legs and ears.

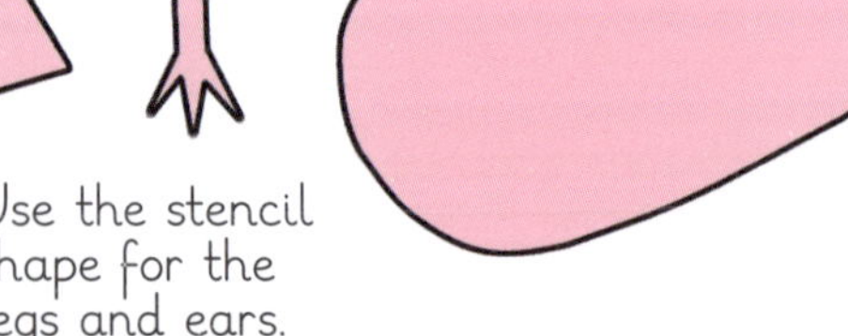

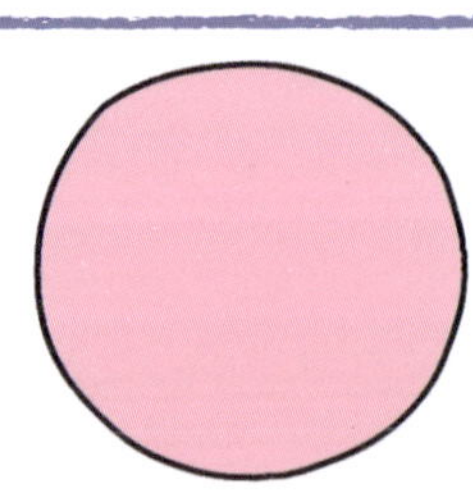

Draw the beak first, and then draw the owl's eyes.

Draw one eye open and the other closed.

Make patterns for the feathers.

Add a tree branch!

Professor owl has a top hat and glasses!

Make your owl look different!

Draw the body the other way for these owls.

Draw a rocking horse

① Draw the horse's head.

② Add the body.

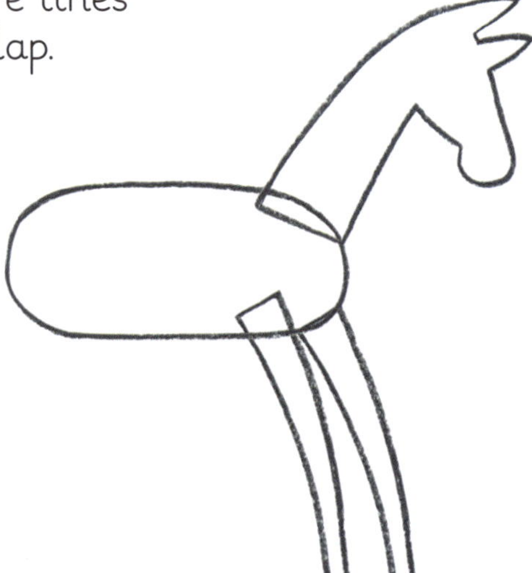

③ Now, draw the front legs.

④ Draw the back legs.

⑤ Add a tail.

Find the horse
pieces at the back
of the book. Set
them out in front
of you like this:.

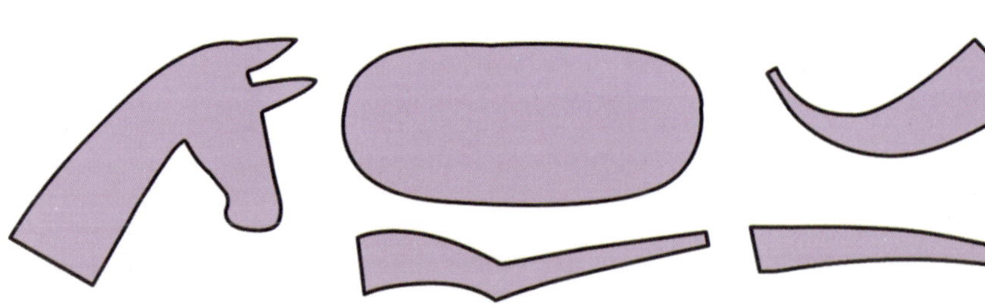

Make a
pretty saddle
with a star.

Draw a mane, too!

Draw along the
edge of a large
paper plate
to create the
rockers.

Make your horse
look different!

Make the horse gallop by
drawing the legs like this.

This horse
is ready for
a show!

Choose
colors you
like for your
horse.

Draw straight
legs.

Draw a super squirrel

Draw lightly where lines overlap.

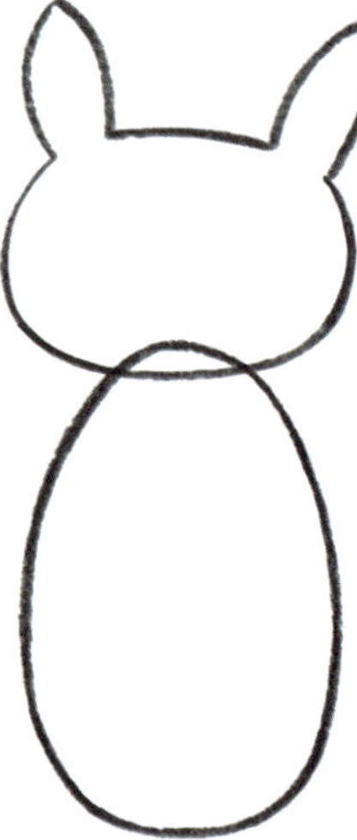

1 Draw the squirrel's head.

2 Now, draw the body.

3 Add the arms and legs.

4 Finally, add a bushy tail.

Find the squirrel pieces at the back of the book. Set them out in front of you like this:

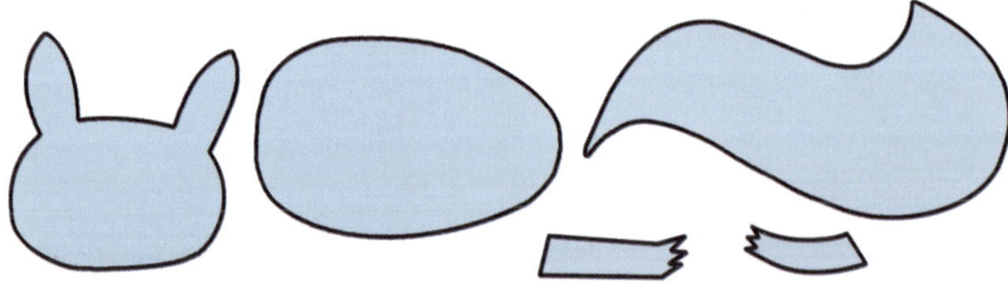

Choose your favorite colors for your squirrel.
Leave white patches on his tummy, face, and ears.
Give your squirrel a tasty acorn in his paws!
Make your squirrel look different!
Tilt the head, and draw closed eyes.
Give your squirrel a flower to smell.
Turn the body around to make this squirrel.

Draw a huge hippo

Draw lightly where
lines overlap.

1 Draw the hippo's head.

2 Add the body.

3 Now, draw the
legs at different
angles.

4 Add a little tail
high up the
hippo's back.

Find the hippo
pieces at the back
of the book. Set
them out in front
of you like this:

Give your hippo a bath by drawing water all around it!
Add a little bird. too!
Make your hippo look different!
You can draw the hippo's mouth open without changing the shape of the head.
Draw closed eyes.
Give your hippo a big smile!
Draw two legs and shift the head to draw this hippo!

Draw a colorful chameleon

Draw lightly where lines overlap.

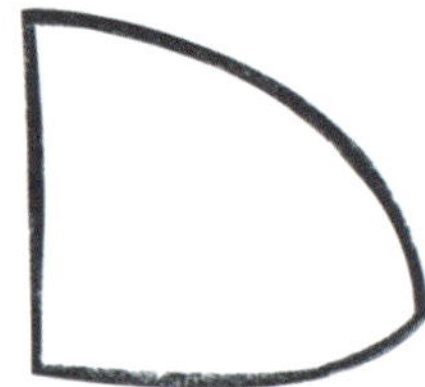

1 Draw the chameleon's head.

2 Then, add the body.

3 Now, draw the legs.

Find the chameleon pieces at the back of the book. Set them out in front of you like this:

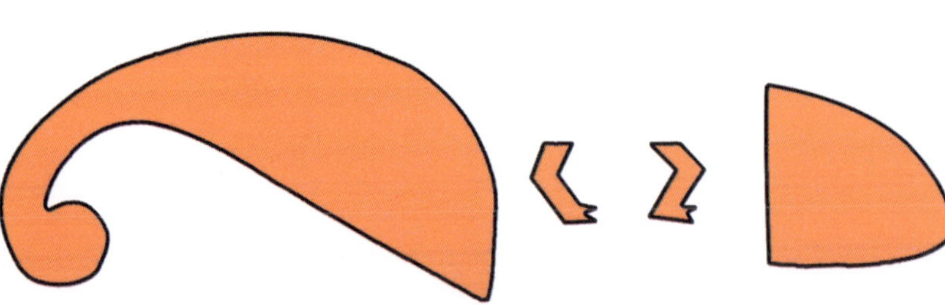

Draw a zigzag of spines along the back.

Draw circles for the eye!

You could draw the eye in a spiral.

Put your chameleon on a branch with some bright green leaves.

Make your chameleon look different!

Add spikes on the head.

Give your chameleon a pattern!

Add a long, sticky tongue to catch lunch!

Chameleons can change color, so create yours using lots of different colors.

Draw a hungry panda

1 Draw the panda's head.

2 Add the body.

3 Now, draw the arms.

4 Draw the legs.

Find the panda pieces at the back of the book. Set them out in front of you like this:

Pandas like to eat bamboo shoots. You could give your panda a nice lunch!

Draw big black circles around the eyes.

Color the arms and legs in black.

Draw claws on the paws!

Make your panda look different!

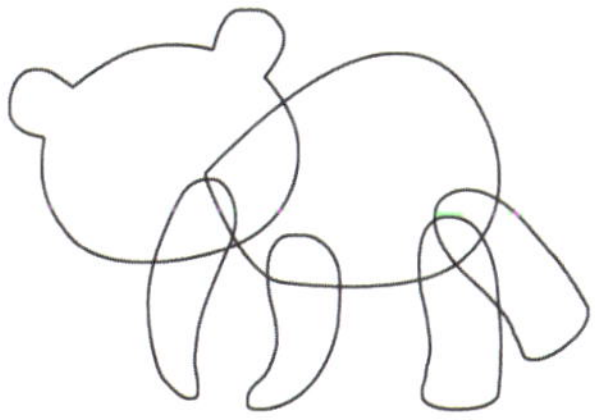

Add a bird!

Give the panda a smile!

Draw a funny monkey

Draw lightly where
lines overlap.

1. Draw the monkey's head.

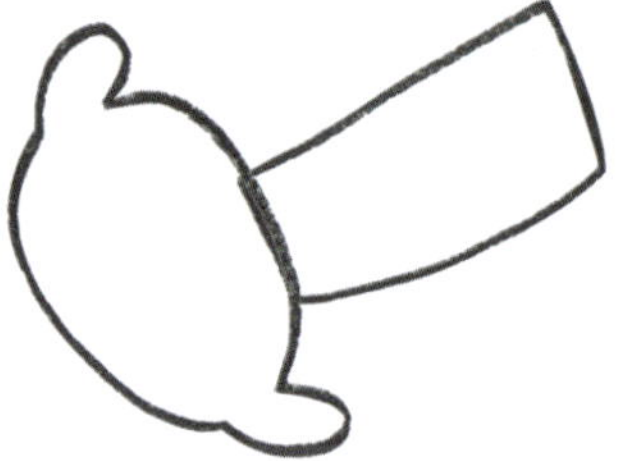

2. Add the body.

3. Now, draw the legs.

4. Draw the monkey's arms.

5. Add a curly tail.

Find the monkey
pieces at the back
of the book. Set
them out in front
of you like this:

Add a buzzing bee!

Draw a tree so your monkey can swing!

You could give
your monkey a hat!

Make your monkey look different!

Choose your
favorite
colors.

Make a
bright
pattern.

How about
a musical
monkey?

Draw a crazy creature!

You can invent your own crazy creature by using shapes to draw around from different animals. Give your creature a funny name. Here's how to draw a Domolibird!

You could draw lots of different crazy creatures by mixing up the shapes to draw around.

Make a display of all the animals you've drawn using this book. Impress your family and friends!